E.M. Sol is an emerging young writer who has honed his craft for the past three to five years, consistently producing poems, short stories, and even novels amidst schoolwork and a busy schedule. This marks his exciting debut as a published author. Fueled by a deep passion for writing, E.M. Sol hopes to share his work with the world and inspire other aspiring writers.

To the lone daisy I found in my garden: may the love I showered upon you guide your path moving forward. If fate allows, may we meet again.

E.M. Sol

TO BE LOVED IS TO BE CHANGED

AUSTIN MACAULEY PUBLISHERS®

LONDON * CAMBRIDGE * NEW YORK * SHARJAH

ISBN – 9789948741015 – (Paperback)
ISBN – 9789948741022 – (E-Book)

Application Number: MC-10-01-4370340
Age Classification: E

The age group that matches the content of the books has been classified according to the age classification system issued by the UAE Media Council.

Printer Name: iPrint Global Ltd
Printer Address: Witchford, England

First Published 2024
AUSTIN MACAULEY PUBLISHERS FZE
Sharjah Publishing City
P.O Box [519201]
Sharjah, UAE
www.austinmacauley.ae
+971 655 95 202

"To Lea, one of the greatest artists I know,
thank you for everything."

1

I look at the stars to try and find you.

in search of beauty, I found you;
in search of home, I found your company.

I take another glance once more at the stars,
only to realize that you were no longer there.

2

My feelings for yous
are like the ocean waves
that come rushing towards the shore

and shy ever so slightly away from it—

you were comparable to the sun;
your peach eyes made the world seem brighter.

3

Do you think things would've changed
if we hadn't met?

Yes, it would have.

4

I see the ocean waves crashing down the beach,
        the soft sand curling and tucking in.

Closure.

          Would things have worked out
          in another life?
     Or maybe in another universe, we'd have stayed the
     same—

Not disconnected from one another,
     drifting apart.

5

13

I have no more words left for others;
no poems left to compose, and no songs left to sing.

For you have taken them all—
just as you have taken my heart.

6

I want to dance under the pouring rain with you,

like the leaves fluttering across the wind.

I want to hold you in my arms.

7

15

You leaving us left a hole in our hearts,

and I was left to put all the pieces back in place,
slowly,
       slowly,
              slowly,
                     slowly, but surely.

8

Loving you was like picking a rose,
despite its thorns;

like staring into the sun,
knowing it would blind me.

9

Instead of helping me tear down the numerous walls
I've surrounded my heart with,
>> you made me put more up.
>>> Perhaps it was because I had
>>> longed for someone to confide in.
>> But this vast void you've left in my heart—
>> my soul, it's something that will,
> like everything else,
numb over time.

10

Looking back
at the fond memories of everyone,

but now,

we've all gone our separate ways,
and I'm left to wonder,

where did all the time go?

11

People come and go,
>   but I'm glad to have met some
>   that have stayed with me
>   through thick and thin.

12

People change like the seasons rolling around.

Perhaps in another life, some other crazy, alternate point in time,

we'd have stayed friends,

    but it just so happens that,
        in this one,

        we didn't.

13

I think of you every second we are apart;

in the back of my mind, it's you.

The words "good morning," "good night,"

when I say them to others, I mean nothing by it,
but when it's to you,

it means you are my first thought when I start the day
and the last as I doze off to sleep.

14

There are days where,

I have so many things to say, so many stories to
speak of to you,

then I remember

that you're no longer in my life.

15

To all my friends,

whether near or far,
across continents, across oceans,
separated by time zones or not,
and whether we're still friends,

always know that I'm thankful for everything
you've all taught me.

Words alone can't express how grateful I am
to have been a part of your lives.

16

I write poems
because I can't express my feelings
through the spoken word.

I feel that
through poetry,
I can speak volumes.

17

You are not defined by your past,

      but rather, who you choose to be right now,
in this moment,

      and who you choose to be
      moving forward.

18

Ever since you left, there's been this big empty
void left in my heart.

Whenever my day starts and the sun rises,
I'd usually wake up in anticipation of you.

And whenever night falls, and the day ends,
I knew I could rest easy knowing you would stay.

But you didn't.

I always have so many things to say to you,
so many stories to tell; so many new poems to show
you.

But now all I can do is to keep them to myself,

in hopes that, if one day, you ever return,
I can tell you all about them.

19

27

Sometimes, I just love staring up at the sky,

because I know that somewhere out there,
   in this big, wide world of ours,

      you're there waiting for me.

20

You will become just a memory,
    endlessly,
        endlessly,
            endlessly,
                replaying in my mind,

longer than I have been your friend.

21

The amount of things I could write about you

are like the stars that fill the night sky:

Endless.

22

I'd take each piece of my heart and soul
and share it with you.

The universe is unkind to us all,
        but if it was for you,
        I wouldn't mind carrying
                a part of that burden.

I speak of you to the moon so often,
        I wouldn't be surprised if it suddenly sang
        a soft melody about you.

23

31

You don't know how much I talk about you
to the moon.

> Whenever I go out for midnight strolls,
> I oftentimes find myself staring at the moon,
> because oh, how much it reminds me of you.

> You shine brighter than every star
> in our galaxy,
> you burn just as passionately as the sunshine during
midday.

> I could replace every star in our galaxy with you,
> and the night skies would still be as pretty—
> Hell, maybe even prettier with you.

24

I still cover my mouth when I burp.

I still take the time to admire the art of whatever it is
I'm reading.

I still sit by the parking lot every so often to
eat strawberry ice cream,
even if you aren't here anymore.

I still buy kinder Buenos because those were your
favorites.

I still do the things I usually do with you or
whenever you're around
because I can't forget—
I don't want to forget.

I don't want you to become
just a memory,

but it seems,
I'm already too late for that.

25

25

Whenever you smile,

the sun goes into hiding,

because that is enough to light up the world
        and brighten up mine.

26

It's bittersweet to think that
of all the universes, that we were friends,

it had to be in this one
where we weren't anymore.

27

35

I think about you more than you realize,
more than I had realized too.

28

Your radiance shows whenever you smile,
the brightest little star my eyes could see;
        and of all the stars I could have set my eyes on, it was
        you.

        If the nights get too dark for you,
I would carry the sun in the palm of my
hands to light the way.

        If the rain pours down on you,
I will shade you
under the warmth of my embrace.

        And if the world gets too heavy,
then consider me Atlas, as I would gladly
take it off your shoulders, and onto mine.

        All of this,
        if it means I could see your smile
        once more.

29

37

In every part of the world,
        in every little corner of the street,
                in every nook and cranny,
I always find myself finding a piece of you.

It's like wherever I go,
        a piece of your soul; of your memory,
        will always be linked to me.

30

Memories are such a bittersweet thing:

One second, I could be reminiscing all the times we spent together,

> and the next, I suddenly remember the hurt you've caused.

> But I can never bring myself to forget,

> not when you meant so much to me.

31

Maybe at first,
it was your beauty that entranced me,
but that's how everything starts, isn't it?

  As time went on, my heart started to hold a special
  place,
    one that was meant especially for you.

  Of all the flowers I stumbled upon in this garden,

  it was but a simple daisy that caught my eye.

  Even through a screen, I could tell
that you were more precious than any other flower,

  my little daisy.

32

It has come to the point where
        I had forgotten what your voice sounded like.
I hoped that it wouldn't turn out like this,

        but maybe it was for the best?
                Perhaps it was fate that lead us to our paths,
                and somehow,
                        ours had to split away.

33

Time is so fast, isn't it?

The leaves, a lush green hue,
now turned orange.

The days, once long,
now, the nights are longer.

You, my best friend,
now, not.

34

If you feel yourself start to wilt,

    don't hesitate to tell me.

I'll water you and give you the warmth of the sun—

anything to see you smile, pretty daisy.

35

Soon, you will have become a memory,

longer than we have been friends.

And yes, you're still a part of my life,

because everywhere I go,
I always find something that reminds me of you.

And that won't change,

because you were my friend.

36

The lights on the street
will never shine as bright as you do.

even in the darkest of nights,
the world shines so bright,

all because of you.

I hope that I too
shine for you
when the night comes and dusk falls,
      because one thing is for certain:

      No matter how bright I shine,
      it's all just a reflection of you.

37

45

In a crowd of people,
you're the first person I'd try to find.

When the world gets too noisy,
I can find solace in you.

38

The world can take what it wants from me,

but the one thing it can't have is my heart,

for mine was already stolen

by the most beautiful daisy.

39

47

You were everything the waves adored;

they would sing songs and hum soft melodies

of all the times you dipped your toes in the water

and the days you softly played with them,

which is why they tend to always come back to the shore

(to you).

40

I will water you with all my warmth
so that you may grow.

And once you've grown,
we can both enjoy and bask
in the warmth of the sun,

hide together and watch the rain,

and enjoy each other's company.

41

How can I write for others
when you've taken all the words from me?

How do I water the other plants
      when you're the only daisy left in my garden?

It's as if fate pulls me towards you; drawing me in to you.

      Like the world wants me to be yours,
      and I already am.

42

I'm a poet,
but anyone can write as I do.

I'm a lover,
but anyone can love as much as I do.

I'm all these things you say I am,
and yet, I'm not yours.

43

If I was an artist,
I'd paint you by my side,

but I'm a poet,
so I can only write of the loveliness
of each breath you take.

44

You are like the sun,
shining down on me,
showering me with warmth.
> If it was for you,
>> I'd pull the clouds apart
>> just to see the sun.
>> I'd tell the moon to hide just a bit longer
>>> if it meant seeing you,

> because you are a joy to the world—
a joy to me,
>> and everyone deserves
>> to feel the warmth of the sun on their skin,

> just as I have.

45

I hate how I love so much,

Because I fall for the tiniest bit of affection given to me—
I give so much to a person who gives so little to me.

I love like how the moon adores the sun; like how
the sea always finds its way back to the shore.

It's like, once I've grabbed onto something,
I just can't seem to let go.

Sometimes it even feels as if I'm
grasping onto nothing.

I've always loved too much.

Sometimes it scares me
how watering a plant too much
could cause it to wilt away.

46

You say you aren't pretty,
But you're gorgeous, darling.

I have conversations with the moon when I go out for walks
at night,
> and each time, without fail, I spend the whole night
> just talking of how wonderful you are,

> and how, when I see you, it's like I'm looking at a
small
> assortment of flowers.

> Words can't describe how beautiful you are;
> it's as if words from the dictionary aren't enough
> to be able to describe your loveliness.

47

55

They asked me,
"How long would you wait for her?"

Watch as time flies by,
      and all my books and poems throughout my life
      be about her.

48

It's surprising how I just never seem to get tired of you.

It's like just talking to you refreshes my mind,
> puts me at ease,
> and all my worries just seem to float away.

And whenever I see you,
it's as if I'm staring at a painting—
> I just can't seem to find the right words to
> describe you because nothing in the dictionary
> matches how lovely you are.

49

When I look at you, it's like staring at the stars—
I'm always just at a loss for words.

I start to stutter and everything I want to say
just gets lumped up and stuck in my throat,

because it's hard not to appreciate your beauty
when you are everything God made perfect in this world.

And wherever you go, the flowers seem to bloom
and the butterflies dance in joy and glee,
       and the moon starts singing songs about you.

50

I've seen many sunsets,
but looking into your eyes is better.

> I've seen the moon all my life,
> but all my life, never did I know that there was
> something more beautiful.

The moon, the stars, the sun—
> they all pale in comparison to you,
> because when you smile, sunshine
> clouds my thoughts,
> and when you look at me, my heart flutters
> just as the stars do.

51

51

I have forgotten what it meant to be lonely
because you were always there to fill the void.

Now that you've left,
I'm always stuck with so many things to say at the end of each
day,
but then I remember—you aren't there anymore.

52

No amount of
>poems,
>>words,
>>>and love songs

will ever be enough to capture your heart.

53

61

I'm tired of hearing the phrase "Maybe in another life,"

because why couldn't it have been this one?

I just wish I'd be chosen for once,

and not just an option.

54

You are as beautiful as the orange hue
emanating from the sun on the windows of buildings.

I write poems about the moon and the stars
       because you are an existence even more beautiful
       as they are.

I sing songs at night to the moon to let it know
that you are a treasure worth waiting for.

55

Wherever you tread,

flowers bloom,

birds sing,

stars align,

and the rain stops,

because wherever you walk, love follows,
and it just so happened that I was walking beside you.

56

Maybe it's not that I'm always looking for love,

but rather,

I'm always falling into places where love flows.

57

Whenever I think of you, my heart flutters.

Sometimes, while I'm walking,

I stop to think—

> To think about how beautiful the sky is,
> and how lovely the weather is,
> and always, in the back of my mind, I think of you.
>
> Most of the time I don't even remember why
> I'm walking around so aimlessly, but one thing I do know
> is that whenever I do so, you always manage to slip
> into my thoughts.

> but I don't mind.

After all, you are my favorite:
thought,
person,
> *memory,*
> *and love.*

58

I will love you beyond death,

because forever writing in my books are poems about you,

and even as I fade and become one
with the stardust and the earth,

the moon will always watch over you, just as I do.

59

I love you.

And not for any profound, complicated reasons,

but rather, I love you like how I love walking in the morning
and seeing the sun shining down on me—

         like how I love reading.

    My reasons for loving you were never any of
    those complex things.
    I just loved you because you were yourself,

and that's all that ever mattered to me.

60

Will you ever think of me
the way I thought of you?

61

You were like the sun to me.

I felt your warmth whenever you were around,
and my surroundings suddenly shined brighter
than I thought it did.

But now,
I must let you go.

I still find bits and pieces of you wherever I go,
whether that be in

places,

things,

or people.

62

I still love you like how the winds carry
the ocean songs across the waters,

    like how the snow slowly falls into the
    warmth of my hands,

        like how the sea always finds its way
        back to the shore,

            like how the moon will always
            need the sun,

                like how I loved you before.

63

Nothing is permanent,
    (and yet everything stays).

    We hold people so close to our hearts,
        yet when they leave, it's the
        memories that stay,
            (even though we wished *they* would
            stay),
        and not just become another burning
        photograph
        that holds our memories.

    And so time will pass,
        and they will become just a distant memory,
        longer than we have known them.

72

Feelings sway just as easily as
the seasons changing.

You may have loved me at first,
and I too, loved you,

but as time passed,
the roses I left in your heart
withered away,

and all I am left with are the dead petals
remaining in my heart,
left by you.

65

When you smile you outshine the morning sun

and when you look at me
I see the stars in your eyes.

Whenever I'm with you
it's like I can feel the warmth of the spring
even if it's the middle of winter.

66

You and me,

we're

     slowly

          drifting

              apart.

Maybe it was fate that it's happening all over again,
    at the same time, same reason,
    just a different year.

67

75

Talk to me of your worries,
      and I'll shoulder them for you.

I'm ready to brace the tide if it meant
saving you from drowning.

    For you?
      Of course, anything for you.

68

76

You are someone who would put Aphrodite to shame.

You, who burns brighter than the sun during the day,
and shines brighter than the stars at night.

It's as if the moon fell from the sky and
descended right there before me.

69

There's this word in Filipino,
'Tadhana'.
It translates to fate, or destiny.

And there's a lot of times where I think that
things in life are bound to happen, no matter what—

whether that be meeting new people,
reconnecting with old friends,

or people leaving.

I've always blamed myself when things went wrong,
but now I'm starting to realize that

it might just be *Tadhana*
that brought us together,

and what
drove us apart.

70

Maybe we were fated
    to meet and be with each other early,

because we weren't
    going to grow old together.

71

It's such a great feeling to love,

      because no matter how much it hurts—
            how much I've been hurt—

      I will *always* choose to feel.

      To feel love,
      to feel loved,
      to give others love,

      and just,
to feel.

Because what is the point of our existence
as human beings if we don't feel?

      It's a beautiful thing to feel.

72

We were born to hurt and love:

Love comes from pain,
and pain comes from love.

That in and of itself

      is the very existence and meaning of us
      as humans.

We are creatures that never tire from the hurt, from the pain,
and tirelessly,
      endlessly give out love.

        It is in our nature
        to hurt one another,
          to love,
            to feel.

Because that
is what makes us human.

73

To be loved is to be changed.

We were born:
    to love,
        to hurt,
            to feel,
                and to change.

There's this burning fire within all of us.
For some it burns with
    passion;
for others, it burns with
    lingering regrets;
and for a lot, it burns with
    love.

What are we, if not creatures meant to love?
    It is that very same love that changes us;
    molds us into different people—
        more complete versions of ourselves.

And when we lose that love,
    we break into pieces.
Up to us to mend, and put each piece:

Slowly,
> *slowly,*
carefully,
> *carefully,*
gently,
> *gently,*
back together again,
> until we can be whole again.